S0-ASL-087

The Seven Lessons

A Gentle Guide to Embracing Change

A Collection of Personal Stories by

Jessica E. Smith

The Seven Lessons; A Gentle Guide to Embracing Change
©Copyright 2016 Jessica E. Smith. All Rights Reserved

Cover Flower Illustrations by Arlene Kelley
Lotus Illustration by Ashlie Cullins
Author's Photograph by Erin Kroll Photography

Paperback: 978-1-946005-99-1
Hardcover: 978-1-946005-96-0
Ebook: 978-1-946005-98-4

HAWKEYEPUBLISHERS.COM

To my mother:

You continue to guide,
embrace, and inspire everyone around you.

Thank you for being the light.

What a beautiful
life you got to live -
Keep showing up!
♡ - Jessica

Keep in mind...

This is a short collection
of personal stories, lessons,
and reflections from my own journey.
They are invitations for you to peacefully
handle life's many challenges, and
gracefully accept its
many blessings.

It is not my place
to tell, advise, or instruct anyone
as to what they "should do" in any situation;
I am not certified to do that. I simply
share my story in hopes that
it enriches yours.

Be Well.

Jessica Smith

Contents

Introduction

Share your story.

"We are, as a species, addicted to story. Even when the body goes to sleep, the mind stays up all night, telling itself stories." —Jonathan Gottschall

We all have a beautiful story to share. Don't ignore or disregard your story; own and embrace it. All too often we hide our truths from others because we are fearful they might judge us, think less of us, or "unfriend" us. And as we grow older, we forget how much we are actually comforted by story-sharing. Just ask any child what they want to do before bedtime, and their answer would likely be, "Tell me a story!"

1

The fixed routine of a bedtime story has a relaxing effect. The soothing voice of the person telling the story allows for a calm atmosphere in which the child can more easily fall asleep. This emotional response creates a bond between the storyteller and the listener.

There is always someone struggling with the same challenges you are going through; you are never alone.

We would be much kinder to one another if we all wore a sign that signified our current challenge in life. Can you imagine meeting someone and, as they introduce themselves, they share their name as well as their current struggles with you? Bob: cancer patient; Pat: depressed; Shawn: just lost a parent; Emily: homeless; Connie: cat just died; Mary: bullied at school; Carla: spouse just asked for a divorce; Mark: no promotion at work; etc.

Though not always verbalized or seen by the naked eye, this is true of everyone in your life. Look deeper when you meet someone, and especially when you're tempted to judge them. Look into their hearts and understand the unique challenges that we all face.

Embrace your truth by sharing your triumphs, your challenges, and your personal stories. People heal through emotional sharing and by learning from other people's experiences. When you take the time to share your story in a respectful and mature way, others will learn from your experiences. You are right where you need to be at this very moment. And you must have needed every single day of your journey to get to where you are today.

My wish is for you to share your story, embrace the changes in your life, and welcome the lessons from your experiences.

We meet people for a reason. Everyone who crosses our path is a teacher in some way. Life experiences have the ability to teach us, but only if we are ready, willing, and receptive enough to pay attention.

That which causes you anger is teaching you compassion and forgiveness; the things you cannot control are teaching you to let go; and challenges teach you patience.

Just look around you and embrace the lessons!

Lesson 1

Listen to those who do not speak

Embrace animals

"He is your friend, your partner, your defender, your dog. You are his life, his love, his leader. He will be yours, faithful and true, to the last beat of his heart. You owe it to him to be worthy of such devotion." —Unknown

Many years ago I cared for a beloved pet in agony. I could have never imagined the emotions that such an experience would trigger: holding a living entity in my arms like that, and having the responsibility to decide whether to end its suffering or prolong the agony. You must think clearly and efficiently in order to make the right call, and then be able to live with that decision without any regret.

Suffering such a loss can be traumatic, devastating, and life-altering.

Fifteen years ago, when I was a student at the University of Maine at Farmington, my two roommates and I came across a kitten taking shelter in an abandoned car. We didn't know where he had come from or if he belonged to anyone, but we agreed that if he is still in that car three days later, we would take him home to our apartment.

As promised, we gently lifted him out of the abandoned vehicle on the third day, brought him home, and named him Skylar.

After shopping for cat-caring essentials, we returned to the apartment and found our new pet lounging in the living room. We had no idea if he had already been trained to use a litter box, but as soon as we placed the box in the middle of the room, he knew exactly what to do. In that moment we discovered his intelligence and the patience he would show us over the years.

Skylar and I spent a lot of time together and grew closer during my Sophomore year. I took him to the veterinary clinic for his regular checkups, and made sure he got all the necessary shots. At the end of that year, when my roommates and I split up, we agreed that I would take Skylar with me.

The next year I decided to adopt another kitten to keep Skylar company. I named him Bailey, weighing just one pound and nine ounces, and Skylar (then a year old), immediately took Bailey under his care.

When I graduated from college in 2004, my personal reward for graduating and finishing an internship was adding a dog to our lovely pet family. But it wasn't going to be just any dog, I had a very specific and special dog in mind.

Back when my father was part of the military police in the Air Force, his police dog was a German Shepherd. I remember my dad speaking so highly of the breed's loyalty, protection, and love, and I decided back then that I wanted a German Shepherd to one day be my first dog.

I lost my father while I was in college, so adopting a German Shepherd was not only the fulfillment of a lifelong dream, but a way of honoring and connecting with my dad as well.

When I got Logan he was only eight weeks old but already full of life and love. He was extraordinary from the very beginning: neither aggressive nor hyper. He was gentle, kind, calm, and extremely loyal. His eyes were full of innocence and wonder, and whatever I went through during the next ten years, Logan was there.

That's ten years of him greeting me at the door, listening to my stories, and remaining loyal through it all.

These three animals (Skylar, Bailey and Logan) have stuck with me and supported me through many years of turmoil (moves, children, and numerous environmental stressors). It used to soothe me to watch my two cats grooming one another, keeping each other warm, and expressing such love. Skylar would often "talk" with his human companions using various vocal tones. He followed me from room to room, and had a very high tolerance for my son's playful nature.

As life moved on, my three friends did too. I knew the inevitable was approaching, and Skylar was the first to leave on his next journey. After a week of him not being himself (he experienced increased thirst, lethargic behavior, and decreased socialization); I knew it was time to call the vet.

After eight hours at the clinic, numerous bags of IV fluids, and various medications, it was clear that Skylar was not going to recover. He had kidney failure and a blocked bladder, causing his body to shut down.

The decision to euthanize him because of his pain and discomfort weighed heavily on my conscience. But when the vet brought him into the exam room, Skylar's agony was so clear, making my only choice obvious. His eyes peered up at me while he panted and twitched, communicating in the only way he could that he was ready to go.

I apologized to him repeatedly for making this decision, prayed that he agreed with me, and thanked him for making my life easier during all those years. Skylar always had a way of comforting me when I was crying, and he sensed so much with other humans as well.

After making the difficult decision to say goodbye, the vet told me that Skylar went peacefully and quickly; a sign that it was meant to be. Leaving the vet's office without Skylar weighed heavily on my soul and left a huge lump in my throat. When we got home, Bailey was terribly lost and confused; it was heartbreaking to see. But just as children teach us resiliency, so do animals.

Life will continue to bring about difficult and sometimes unfathomable periods of adjustment, but Skylar's picture will forever remain in a beautiful frame on the windowsill of our kitchen. His name is still spoken in our home with love and light, and we proudly share his story with everyone who comes to visit.

Over the next few years, Logan and Bailey continued to emotionally support me, my family, and one another.

One year, during an exceptionally hot morning in August, my husband and I noticed our dog Logan was pacing and acting uncomfortable. We prepared a special breakfast for him, which he practically inhaled, but vomited all over the living room floor an hour later.

I put Logan in the backseat of the car, and we rushed to the emergency clinic. He rested in the backseat with a tarp under him, ever so quiet and noticeably sad. I wondered if he knew where we were going. I just kept talking to him, comforting him. There was no radio, no distractions, just us. I whispered sweet stories to him about our shared experiences together over the years, and I tried reassuring him that everything was going to be okay.

When we arrived at the clinic, we sat together in the hallway, waiting for a private room that would ultimately become our last place to exchange kisses, warm embraces, and loving prayers. I could feel he was nervous, and I was nervous, too. When the doctor greeted us in the hallway, Logan peed on the floor, shivering, yet wagging his tail. I just kept stroking his thick mane and speaking to him ever so calmly. We walked slowly into exam room number 4, and the door closed behind us.

Logan was diagnosed with a very serious autoimmune disorder (his system could no longer differentiate the good bacteria from the bad, and his internal bleeding was out of control). He appeared happy on the outside, but he had sadness in his eyes, as if to say, "It's okay, Momma, it's time to let me go."

I sat on the floor with him, feeling my inner child surface, and I cried uncontrollably. That's when I heard someone in the hallway say, "Go ahead, they're in room number four."

My husband, son, and daughter came into the room, and Logan started wagging his tail. We were all crying, arms wrapped tightly around Logan's neck, never wanting to break that circle.

Logan grew to be 116 pounds of greatness before he passed. He watched over me through the years; witnessing my growth, striving to reach my goals, and creating the little family we now have. He protected it. He was extraordinary and one of a kind. He was my first dog, and he left a lasting impression on our little family. Logan was an inspiration, as all dogs are, with their loyalty, non-judgmental attitude, dedication, and daily faithful greeting at the door.

Logan must have heard me tell my friends that I really wanted him to make it to the milestone of his tenth birthday, because he crossed the rainbow bridge that night, just a month after turning ten.

The vet gave me plenty of time with Logan, but it never felt long enough. I kissed Logan's nose, cheeks, and my favorite spot right between his eyes. That was *my* spot.

Crying, trying to catch my breath, I finally said to him, "I'm so sorry for the pain you were in. My love for you is endless and eternal. Thank you for being my savior, my guide, and my best friend. Thank you. Thank you. Thank you. God, I love you."

And that was the last time I ever saw him.

Arriving home from the clinic that night, and opening the front door to be greeted by silence instead of Logan, was an awful reminder, smacked in my face, that life had changed once again.

My husband brought Logan's ashes home a week later, and we laid him to rest in my perennial flower garden, where he loved to be.

Although no longer a kitten, Bailey is still the baby in the family. He never grooms himself like Skylar used to; he just goes with the flow and has a tiny, innocent meow.

Bailey is still part of our family, turning 14 this year. He has lost two of his best friends, but has warmly welcomed two new pet members into our home without skipping a beat.

I continue to learn from Bailey and his peaceful nature, maturity, and openness to accept change. I know the inevitable day of his passing is growing near, but for the time being, we snuggle daily, and I remain grateful for his presence and friendship. Bailey is a beautiful example of embracing change; he gracefully lives his life as everything around him continues to shift, and he does it effortlessly while purring up a storm.

Admire and respect these amazing, furry beings with whom we are so lucky to share our lives.

→ Embrace animals ←

Learn the valuable lessons presented by your pets and the animals that surround you every day. Embrace everything and every living creature in your path as a teacher. Animals offer unconditional love and support without expecting anything in return. They exude an admirable life of simplicity, and they require very little to be happy: a few toys, some food and water, a warm bed, and lots of love. That's it. Could you live with these simple things?

Animals find pure joy in playing fetch, the pat of a hand, or the simple act of a door opening and their beloved companion coming home. Their lifestyle, their love language, and their giving nature, are all to be admired and honored.

Observe your four-legged friends and notice their compassion, patience, and loyalty in every situation.

Have you ever watched a focused dog? They sit quietly, listen to their surroundings, and fully assess situations before reacting.

So listen carefully. Observe your surroundings. Live in the moment. Animals do not plan anything, and we can learn from them.

Animals do not worry about their future or about their struggles like humans do. We get caught up in the past or future, and we lose sight of the now. Learn this valuable lesson from your pet: to live in the now, soak up the sun, and chase that ball.

Hug your pet today, adopt a pet, and learn from the animals in your life. Listen to their unspoken language, look into their eyes, and feel the love they have for you. It's all for you. Love as loyally and as fully as they do.

Lesson 2

Save Sisterhood

Embrace friendship

"The ones who notice the storms in your eyes, the silence in your voice, and the heaviness in your heart, are the ones you need to let in." —Steve Maraboli

Simple yet complicated question: why do we gossip about one another?

Judgment, gossip, and bullying are hurtful ways of sharing. Every one of us has been gossiped-about after divulging intimate information with others; it hurts. These incidents not only hurt our feelings but trigger apprehension about the next time we want to share from the heart. It takes courage to trust another person with intimate details about your personal story.

Trust is defined as "a firm reliance on the integrity, ability, or character of a person or thing."

Gambling is defined as "to bet on something uncertain, or to stake something on a contingency; to take a chance."

To trust another person is to gamble. Many of us struggle with trusting one another for various reasons, so we end up keeping our thoughts and feelings to ourselves. Trusting in others is a challenge if you've been disappointed or betrayed in the past. To embrace change, however, and actually welcome challenges that force you to personally grow, is a way to let go of the anger that a mistrusting situation left you with.

One day in early June, I was a few months shy of turning twenty-four years old, about to start a new career: my first job that paid an annual salary, offered medical benefits, required an adult wardrobe, and allowed me to use my acquired education. There was no turning back as I took the exit off the freeway to my new office; this was it. I pulled into the parking lot of this massive building, and felt very small and young. I opened the glass doors and greeted the receptionist: "Hi, I'm Jessica. I'm here for my first day in the children's case management office; it's upstairs, correct?"

"Hi there!" She said. "Go on upstairs and turn right; the secretary will direct you to your office. And good luck!"

I felt a knot in the pit of my stomach as I watched employees walking by me, busy on their cell phones with their name tags swinging back and forth, everyone in such a rush. I walked up the stairs, looked up at the sunshine streaming through a beautiful skylight, took a deep breath, and opened the door. I had no idea that I would end up spending six years working at this office, learning, growing, embracing change, and helping families in need.

Earlier that month a few case workers were transferred elsewhere, so I was assigned a nice, corner cubicle. I felt like I was in grade school again and had that "new girl" look. A bit apprehensive and quiet most of the morning, I only asked the questions I needed answered in order to gain some knowledge of the job, but ultimately kept to myself.

At that time in my life I was an introvert who had grown to love solitude. I was in a terrible relationship, which left me feeling unworthy and unlovable. If I was alone, without friends, I didn't have to answer any questions about my bad relationship or hear any unwanted opinions. But the hurt was visible and the fear was noticeable.

I found myself increasingly nervous and afraid to open up to anyone around me, especially women. Thoughts about being judged overwhelmed me: Will women look down on me and see me as a failure? Will I be gossiped about? Will they secretly smile because I am experiencing hardship? My own judgments and preconceived thoughts were taking over my mind, preventing me from processing and letting go of what needed to be released.

Two cubicles down from me, I could hear a woman's voice speaking softly to a client on the phone. She was gentle and careful not to repeat too many details aloud in order to respect the client's privacy. She hung up the phone, walked over to my cubicle, and said, "Hi! Are you ready to be overworked and underpaid?" She let out a loud laugh and quickly sat down next to me.

That "grade school" feeling came rushing in again, this time igniting friendly thoughts within: I like her. Maybe she wants to hang out. She's nice.

As we talked, she showed me around the workplace and let me in on all the secrets of the office life. She was one of the nicest people I had ever met.

In the beginning of our friendship, we sometimes found it hard to relate to one another: she had a husband and children, and I was unmarried with pets. Her time away from work was filled with after-school activities, and mine was filled with either shopping or hiking with Logan. But she always managed to find subjects we could both relate to. She made my life feel just as important as hers, even though we were on completely different paths at the time.

One morning she came into work looking frazzled, with sadness clearly visible in her eyes. I asked if she was okay, gently touched her shoulder, and said, "I'm here for you. Let's go downstairs to the cafeteria and talk for a bit. The office meeting doesn't start for another hour."

She looked away, turned on her computer, and said, "I can't, Jess. I just can't right now. Sometimes I come to work to escape the stress of home, so let's just talk about something else."

I respected her feelings and swiftly changed the subject. The conversation turned positive as I began to share with her a reflective piece I had been writing. Her face beamed as she read it, eyes shining with delight; it was captivating to watch. She turned to me, her face as bright as a sunrise, and said, "Jess, this is so beautiful. Wow, I am so honored you allowed me to read this. Thank you so much. I am just so happy for you."

Not only was she genuinely happy for me, the words she spoke seemed to somehow smile. Her facial expression, her body movements, and her words all beamed with light and happiness, which I felt deep down in my heart. No woman had ever talked to me with pure love and genuine happiness like that before. She not only said the words, but she had an amazing way of letting me *feel* her words. And that, to me, is priceless. It was in that moment that I realized I was not only looking at a forever friend, but a true soul sister.

Through all of life's changes, she has been a friend for me to laugh with and a shoulder to cry on. She kept me grounded when I got a promotion, and helped me reassemble my self-worth when I was going through a difficult breakup.

Our social circle quickly grew as we shared our stories and embraced other women. Encouraging smiles, a gentle touch to a shoulder, and simple reminders of our worth were small steps toward sisterhood.

Human beings are remarkable in general, but in my opinion, women are just pure, divine, and amazing. The way we unintentionally carry ourselves through life with grace is pretty astonishing, and yet we all hide behind a wall sometimes. The reasons behind the walls we put up greatly vary, but the walls are generally covered in words like judgment, fear, attachment, comparison, competition, and gossip.

We feel the need to protect ourselves, compare, judge, and compete with one another. Let's stop letting toxic words like comparison and competition leak into our minds to justify judgments. Hardship and gossip have left us with the impression that other women are the enemy, and that simply isn't true.

We've all been hurt, betrayed, and judged. And although the reasons for our pain fade with time, the scars remain. Be it emotional or physical pain, it's all traumatic, and yet we're still here at the end of the day. We have overcome everything that was put in our path so far, and that is pretty remarkable.

It was the sisterhood that guided me to embrace myself as a beautiful individual, and to embrace my own unique story.

Embrace being *you*. It's possible to admire a trait in someone else (like their beauty, elegance, posture, or grace), without degrading or questioning your own. It's okay to admire and want to become friends with women because of their amazing qualities or fascinating stories.

I often feel connected to women on a soul level because of how they make me feel. Don't think that you can't stand to be around someone simply because they remind you of everything you are not, and don't compare their life to yours. Get those negative thoughts out of your mind.

You have within you the ability to be genuinely happy for another woman's success. Go ahead and empower other women because we are all beautiful and strong in our own way—you simply need to find what makes *you* shine.

Ask other women what inspires them, and invite them to tell you how they conquer certain challenges in life. Women are triumphant warriors who ought to be encouraged to share the lessons they have learned without fear, without shame, and without judgment.

Friendship is scary. Sisterhood is scary. It's a risk, but one worth taking with beautiful benefits.

Sisterhood is instinctive, knowing what's wrong without asking. Sisterhood is fierce, protecting your tribe and respecting you. Sisterhood is real, with a swift nudge that you sometimes need to help you realize your life isn't as bad as you think it is. Sisterhood is raw, pure honesty and genuine comfort. Sisterhood is deep, a soulful connection that often feels indescribable. Sisterhood is trust, knowing your secrets are safe, always accepting your questionable choices in life. Sisterhood is priceless, worthy of the risk in sharing your story.

It has been ten years since the beginning of my soul sister experience. We still talk every day, have a flourishing relationship, our children play together, and our support for one another will never fade. I am forever grateful for that cubicle in the corner, on that hot summer day ten years ago.

My wish is for you to find your tribe, share your story, and be with soul sisters who always keep you smiling.

⇢ Embrace friendship ⇠

Learn from the women in your life. Share your story with other women, and get excited about finding your tribe.

Women were created for community. We hold within us the power to embrace one another and create a loving community for all. When you surround yourself with other women, you will find yourself becoming a better partner, a better mother, and a better person all around. We have an amazing ability to nurture one another and provide an empathic presence.

Support sisterhood by encouraging one another. There is power in sisterhood; a sacred and historical bond, where we can bare our souls and feel at ease.

Think about this: many years ago, women raised their children with the help of everyone in their village. They worked together to prepare huge meals for their communities, helped one another, and leaned on one another when the stress of home life grew unmanageable. Why did we ever lose this supportive, encouraging fellowship? When did commonalities and community become competition and isolation?

Let's bring sisterhood back. Let's bring friendship back. Let's bring community back.

Be brave enough to start a deep conversation that matters; one that is soulful, real, and kind. Feel what happens when you connect with other women; it is an indescribable feeling, and one you are all worthy of experiencing.

Because of social media, comparison and competition are two words that have taken on a whole new meaning, especially among women who are constantly comparing their lives to someone else's. Don't minimize your own happiness by envying the happiness of others. No one is a stranger to loneliness, anger, hurt, or fear. No one is spared grief or loss in this life. No one.

If you are enjoying a relaxing afternoon, and you happen to see someone sitting on a beach in the park, lounging on their yacht, or waiting at the airport to depart toward a lavish destination, do not compare. Just enjoy where you are in that moment and *who* you are in that moment. No one else can play your role in this game we call life. You are wonderful just the way you are, and you are right where you need to be. Truly believe this: you are exactly where you are supposed to be.

It's important to notice where you focus your time, energy, and attention. The people you surround yourself with have a huge impact on your attitude and a profound influence on who you will become. Surround yourself with individuals who respect themselves and their relationships; individuals who inspire and motivate you to be the best version of you there is.

It's been said that we become like the five people we spend the most time with, so be sure to surround yourself with true soul sisters.

You are worthy of being surrounded by people who want nothing more than amazing things for you. When you find women who do not compete, who stick by you during happiness and sadness, and who support your crazy dreams, then you have found your tribe. Love them hard because strong women build each other up.

You deserve to be supported, loved, and defended. You deserve the world. You deserve true and fierce soul sisters.

Lesson 3

Less judgment, more kindness

Embrace kindness

"We can judge others or we can love others, but we cannot do both at the same time."   —Unknown

Life becomes more demanding as we get older, and it offers many opportunities for us to learn, forgive, and grow. Learning to forgive is a challenge in and of itself; you have to be fully engaged and know in your heart, mind, and soul that forgiving will facilitate growth.

The most difficult and important lesson in forgiveness came to me when I was eighteen years old and my father took his own life. I was just a young woman; a freshman in college and not at all prepared to emotionally process what happened.

There are times when I feel lost in the pain of missing him. I am left with a feeling of abandonment that no one can explain or understand; hovering between confusion and anger, where the feelings completely consume me. Losing my father in a traumatic way has shown me just how deeply I can feel, how hard I can fall, and how grief can consume my entire being at times. It has also taught me how forgiveness can heal, and how I can help others so that they do not suffer the way my father did.

He was a military man who struggled with severe depression and Post Traumatic Stress Disorder. My dad desperately sought a place to feel at home in this world. He tried to find comfort in his adopted family, he tried to find courage by joining the Air Force, and he tried to find understanding by becoming a father. He was a quiet soul who was socially awkward in a sweet and innocent way. His eyes radiated sadness, and he tried desperately to express his love for his family without actually verbalizing it. He thought of me as too sensitive and would often preach life lessons in hopes of "toughening my skin" before sending me out into the big, scary world. He ultimately and unintentionally taught me the hardest lesson of all: how to forgive and embrace change.

It was Monday, February 19th, a date by which I now measure time in my life: everything either occurred before that date or after.

I awoke that morning, drove south for a few hours to a friend's house, and fell asleep on her couch shortly after arriving. Then, around 9:00 p.m. there was a knock at the door. My friend got up to answer it, and found a priest standing there next to a Maine State Trooper.

As I sat up on the couch, they walked into the living room, and my heart started pounding wildly. My friend's face was unexpectedly pale, and she couldn't look at me. They entered the living room, and I began to scream, "What happened? Why are you all looking at me like that?" It was one of those moments where you hear yourself ask the questions aloud, but you ultimately dread the answers.

The trooper slowly took his hat off and firmly yet quietly said, "I'm sorry to tell you this, Jessica, but your father has died."

The priest quickly intervened, sat down on the ottoman in front of me, and softly added, "He died quietly, in his sleep, with his cat next to him. He took his own life, my dear, by overdosing on medication, but he's at peace now."

Time stopped. My heart stopped. The pounding in my ears stopped. I can't even recall what they said next. I don't remember what I did after that. I just remember hearing questions fading in and out: "Did you know he was ill?" "Maybe this is a good thing considering the circumstances?" "Do you want to go see your mom now?" It's all a blur.

I didn't just cry, I sobbed like never before, shaking to the point where passing out would have felt better. It was like a dream or a sad movie, not at all like real life. It certainly didn't feel like *my life.*

The trooper handed me his business card and the pastor's phone number, but I had to wipe my tears away to focus on what I was holding.

"Here is our contact information," he said. "If there is anything you need, or if you ever need to… just talk… please don't hesitate to call us. I cannot even imagine what you are feeling right now."

This strange man in uniform, whom I barely knew, comforted me tremendously that evening with his calming presence and soft tone. It took immense reassurance on my part, but the police officer and priest finally agreed to leave.

My friend and I packed a few bags, drove through the night, fueled by caffeine and fast food, and finally arrived up north in the early morning hours. As we drove into our friends' driveway, my mother greeted us at the front door, weeping. I collapsed into her arms and took a deep breath.

The next morning the funeral planning swiftly began, and life as I knew it would never be the same.

I remember feeling awkward and out of control. I worried about the stigma attached to the way he died, along with the potential judgment, the unfamiliar pain, and the unknown future. What looks will I get upon returning to the university? How will people act around me? Am I a statistic? Am I a survivor? My mind raced. My feelings cycled through anger, resentment, betrayal, confusion, and hurt. How could he do this to me and our family? Didn't he want to see me graduate from college, get married, have children? Why leave me with all these questions? This guilt? This pain? Why would he do such a thing, take the easy way out and refuse any help? He was such a great father, a strict Catholic, a military man. Why would he do this?

Then I realized that all my pain and all of my questions revolved around *me*. Not him. My inner victim was loud and self-pitying. And that's part of the problem. People who experience intense pain from deep depression or mental illness aren't thinking rationally. My dad wasn't thinking about my wedding in the future, the grand kids he would have, or his next vacation. He was simply in pain— unbearable, unmanageable pain that he couldn't escape. He needed help. But people turned away because it was uncomfortable to reach out, or perhaps because they thought it wasn't their problem, or that he was just mean.

My father was an amazing man who carried valuable lessons with him. He taught the value of hard work by serving twenty years in the United States Air Force, he taught respect by being a man of his word, and he taught compassion by always placing an extra chair at the dinner table for someone who needed a home-cooked meal. We all have a story, but his story is one worth sharing; it is raw, honest, informative, and admirable.

We all have the power to recognize pain in others and offer compassion instead of judgment. In doing so, we can help those in need instead of drawing mistaken conclusions about them and writing them off. Let go of the assumption that only the people talking to themselves on the street or strapped into straitjackets are the ones "crazy" enough to take their own lives—or that they aren't worthy of compassion. Everyone is fighting a battle you know nothing about. And everyone processes loss and hardship in different ways. How much you can handle will differ vastly from what someone else can handle.

We are all hurting in some way, perhaps damaged by tragedy. And yet in spite of everything, many of us rise out of bed each morning and put on a smile. Many people appear composed or happy, giving the outside world the impression that they have it all together, only to return home feeling sad and alone. When someone is scared, in that moment, they are vulnerable. Don't dismiss the vulnerable. Instead, offer a helping hand, a smile, strength, or some love. Those who lift others up usually do so because they've been low before. Break the cycle of looking the other way and ignoring those in need. Become a helper, an agent of change, a beacon of light.

Looking back, I feel content about how I received the news of my father's death. I often think about the priest and state trooper, and I am forever grateful for them. Although the event that evening was tragic, their presence was calming and healing. Nothing that night was their fault. It was a prime example of "behind the scenes" activity that we often overlook when we are quick to criticize law enforcement or religious groups. I cannot begin to fathom what they were feeling at that time; driving to an unknown residence, carrying with them the responsibility of delivering devastating news to a young woman.

When my mother heard of my father's passing, she was an emotional wreck. She was five hours north of me that evening, and shortly after she received the news, she went to a family friend for support. The friend was part of the sheriff's department, so they decided to call the authorities down south and have them deliver the news to me because my mother could not bring herself to do it over the phone. When they made the arrangements, they decided to bring a priest along, just in case there were any concerns about the *way* my father died. Although it was strange to have a police officer and a priest show up on the doorstep, it was actually comforting and calming to hear the story from such caring and professional men. I still have their business cards, fifteen years later, in a box where I keep some of my dad's belongings. Someday, possibly, I will gather the courage to contact them, if only to express painless and honest gratitude from my heart, the message of deep appreciation.

⇥ Embrace kindness ⇤

Learn the lessons that strangers can teach you by reducing your judgments and increasing kindness. Help others find the light within themselves by being someone who leads by example. Everyone is going through something—a hard time, a journey, a challenge, a change. Be the person who treats others with respect. Be polite. Share your story. Hold the door open. Smile. Refrain from judgment. Be quick to listen and slow to react. Be the light. Be the reason someone smiles today.

When you shift your focus and understand that everyone has a story, it will help you be more patient, compassionate, loving, and understanding of where they are, how they got there, and why they seem to struggle. Next time you find yourself growing angry or impatient with someone, please remember that we are all dealing with something. It is not always as easy as we think it should be for others (or for ourselves) to overcome certain challenges.

Obstacles were not created overnight, and they will not go away overnight. Choose to encourage those around you. Everyone has a story of change, guidance, or power to offer. Beauty exists everywhere, but do not get distracted by what you see on the surface. With everything in life, there are many layers beyond what the eye sees. There is an entire world of stories, feelings, and lessons to be found.

Look beyond the surface and learn to differentiate what is real from what is being projected. Share your story with others, learn from others' experiences, and do not get distracted by projection. Be honest with yourself, be proud of all of your layers, and be happy in this moment. Always remember there is someone out there who is happier with a lot less than what you have.

The loss of my father, in such an abrupt way, taught me that you never know who may be completely overwhelmed by the depth of their pain. You never know how much you might help just by offering kindness and compassion. After you endure a challenge in life, find that reason to love again, to forgive again, and to simply live again. You can only learn from the past, grow from within, and embrace whatever comes next. Offer help, but be open to receive help as well. It's okay to not be okay once in a while.

When you look into a stranger's eyes and see sadness, or encounter someone in distress, offer kindness. Don't wait for others to be kind to you; show them how to be kind. Don't pre-judge or assume anything about anyone; allow them to tell their own story—and believe them.

Listen with the intent to understand, be present, and give others the space to be themselves. It is not our place to judge others when they experience hardship, and there is no time limit on grief. You cannot rush the grieving process. Time doesn't necessarily heal; time just has a way of helping you become a bit more comfortable with the closure of a particular chapter.

Even though it may be painful, embrace all transitions with an open mind and open heart. Get excited about new chapters in life, and welcome change with open arms. Be grateful for any opportunity to grow, learn, and expand. You never lose; you only win or learn.

You will get through whatever is presented to you because you were given strength for the life you live. When you encounter a difficulty in life, it is time to use all the strength within you, and trust that you will experience every event in the exact way you are meant to.

Remember that you are already whole. The people who love you will (and should) remind you of this every day.

You are strong.

You are complete.

Embrace your journey.

Lesson 4

Always be teaching, always be learning

Embrace motherhood

"Birth takes a woman's deepest fears about herself and shows her that she is stronger than them." —Unknown

All children hold within them a bit of unseen magic; mysterious and angelic tools nestled deep within.

Being a mother is a divine gift, and each day with my two beautiful spirits is a treasure. Motherhood has been a huge honor for me; I feel truly blessed to witness every giggle, tantrum, and new discovery, and to be truly present for them every day.

My children lived in my dreams for countless years before I actually had them, and now I get to gaze into their eyes and touch their little faces every day. I cannot ignore the fact that among the chaos, the routine, the fatigue, and the temper tantrums, I am literally living my dreams. Grateful. Blessed. In love.

Maternal instincts came naturally for me: selflessness, and the giving of love were automatic. I simply emulated what I witnessed growing up.

I am fortunate to have an amazing, selfless, beautiful woman as a mama; one who is caring, open, communicative, supportive, encouraging, and ultimately her children's biggest fan. So many times in my life when thought I couldn't get through something, her beautiful face instantly appeared. My mom continues to have the strength to go through and grow through everything presented to her.

When I was little, my mom always took care of everything with fluidity and grace. She made sure my sister and I had our homework done, ate healthy meals, took us to numerous after-school activities, led our Girl Scout troops, and always tucked us into bed at night. She never seemed frazzled or preoccupied.

Even now she juggles everything in her life with grace, supports others effortlessly, speaks with love, works hard, and takes care of her own mother. She is an amazing nana to our children, volunteers weekly, maintains her two-acre lot, remains active in her spiritual community, and continues to explore her own creative talents; she does everything! And she does it on her own. She never expects an ounce of credit for how amazing she truly is. I admire the hell out of that woman. She was my role model through childhood and still inspires me today; she is a true and gentle leader.

When I was eight my nana gave me a baby doll for Christmas and I named him Adam. I loved that doll from the moment I laid eyes on him. I remember unwrapping the paper and seeing him in the box, which I opened ever so gently to make sure I didn't hurt him. As soon as he was out of the box, I hugged him, kissed his head, and said, "Oh, Nana, I just love him! I'm going to call him Adam."

Adam and I went everywhere together: from the breakfast table to friends' houses and on car rides. When I went to school I was often consumed by sadness, fearing Adam might be lonely without me.

I am a planner by nature. It comforts me to know what is coming next, and to feel some sense of control over any situation. Life, however, has a gentle and beautiful way of reminding me that I can't plan everything.

When it felt like it was the right time in my life to do so, I began planning my first pregnancy. I read everything in existence about ovulation, implantation, and fertilization. In short: if it had to do with hormone levels or ovulation strips, I knew about it. I even began documenting my intense feelings of love and wrote a journal to my unborn child. But one day, while I was at work, reality came knocking with a tough lesson: I felt a strange but intense sensation in my body, somewhere between sharp cramps and an electric shock in my lower stomach. I went into our office bathroom to discover what every pregnant woman fears: blood.

I had no idea what was happening, and I felt very alone. I called my doctor's office right away and said, "I have intense cramps and I am bleeding a little; is this normal? What should I do?" They told me to come in immediately.

The hospital was just down the street from my office, and there I sat, alone in my car in the parking lot, absolutely terrified.

I remember feeling the hot sun on my legs as I sat there shaking with fear. "This can't be happening!" I cried to my friend on the phone, "I am meant to be a mama. I am supposed to share my love, my wisdom, my guidance, and my story with my children."

As I sat on the doctor's table, shaking with fear, I kept fidgeting with the hospital gown, tying and untying the strings with sweaty hands and racing thoughts. Then the door opened.

"What's happening, Doctor? Why does it hurt so bad? Why are my hormone levels fluctuating so much?"

"What's happening, Jessica, is that your body is having a miscarriage. Let's give it a day or two, and your body will naturally pass the baby. If it doesn't, we will discuss the alternatives then. You've done absolutely nothing wrong. This could be because of your history with endometriosis [a disorder in which tissue that normally lines the uterus grows outside the uterus], but sometimes it just isn't meant to be."

Isn't meant to be?! Miscarriage?! What is this doctor talking about? She must have the wrong patient. I planned this so well. She must be wrong.

She wasn't wrong.

I was so sad. I was confused. I was mad. Mad at my body, mad at my partner, and mad at my unborn baby.

A day and a half later, having reached the threshold of my tolerance for excruciating pain, I went back to the hospital and requested an immediate ultrasound. As I lay on the cold table, the technician explained each aspect of the procedure while I peered up at the black and white screen. I was completely engulfed in pain, feeling like something was about to burst inside of me, and saw the technician's face suddenly turn from sadness to fear.

"Oh, my God," she quietly whispered, and then immediately called the doctor. Within seconds a team of nurses and other doctors formed around me, and before I knew it I was signing paperwork.

"Jessica, you are going in for emergency surgery. Who can we contact?"

"Surgery?" I asked. "Now? Like, right now? What's wrong? I thought you said the baby would naturally pass on its own."

I remember counting backwards from ten... nine... eight... and then I was out.

When I awoke my abdomen was sore and I started crying profusely. I remember hearing the nurse whisper to someone, "She's awake. Go get the doctor."

She slowly raised my bed, offered me a tiny amount of water through a straw, and kindly wiped my tears. The doctor explained that I had an ectopic pregnancy, where the baby gets stuck in the fallopian tube, and mine was minutes away from rupturing.

I learned that many women actually die from internal bleeding caused by ectopic pregnancies every year. The doctor described the complexity of the surgery, explaining why they needed to remove the entire tube due to damage, but then quickly reminded me of the positive: that I am fortunate to be alive and still have one working tube. "You're young," she said, "and your left tube will just have to work twice as hard now, and that's perfectly fine! We believe you can still have babies in the future..."

Anything she said after that faded into white noise. I couldn't believe she took my tube out. Oh my God! What happened to the little embryo? What was I to do next? What would I tell the people who knew I was expecting? And my stomach hurt so much.

I was released from the hospital the next day. Completely astounded by this first pregnancy experience, I tried to remain positive and keep trusting my body. Having to say goodbye to this little soul before even having the chance to say hello was a strange and profound experience.

Days passed, weeks passed, and life went back to a new normal. Time, friends, and family helped with the healing process, and keeping a positive attitude was essential. My body not only adjusted, but pleasantly surprised me with a new pregnancy just four months later.

As prepared as I thought I was because of all the books I had read about pregnancy, I honestly had no idea what I was doing. You can read and research until your eyes bleed, but nothing prepares you for motherhood except for the honest and raw reality of it.

I had an amazing pregnancy with my son. I would sit on the edge of the bed with my hands on my lower belly and whisper to him, "Everything is going to be okay, love. You and me. Me and you."

I was proud of my body and so happy to be carrying a little boy. I talked to him, read to him, and even had him listen to classical music in my womb. When I went into labor, I just thought the Mexican food wasn't agreeing with me, I had no idea it was actual labor. Eventually I went to the hospital, and 39 hours later welcomed my son into the world.

And everything changed.

I have never held so much love for a little being in my life before. I was totally connected with this tiny soul, and his simple presence felt healing to me. I loved caring for him and the routine we created at home, and I cherished witnessing all his little milestones.

Years went by, and with them came inevitable life transitions, including a new life partner. We got married, bought our dream home, and while unpacking some moving boxes, we started talking about adding more members to our family.

My doctor said it might be difficult for me to have another baby because of my increasingly progressive endometriosis, but my dream was to have a little girl named Emma.

On my twenty-ninth birthday, my husband and I went out to dinner with some friends. I had one margarita with my meal and instantly felt ill. On the way home we stopped to purchase a pregnancy test, and within seconds of getting home, without even taking my shoes off, I ran to the bathroom to take the test.

It was positive. Not a dull, light mark that leaves you guessing… Is that a line? Could it be? Let me get my magnifying glass… hmm… It wasn't at all like that; this was a very intense, bold, in-your-face, bright line that beamed: "Hello! Here I am!"

I smiled with delight and calculated being only four or five weeks pregnant. I was surprised at how positive the test was; and little did we know, it was an indication of our darling daughter's personality.

Being pregnant with my daughter was incredible. I harbored just a little bit of doubt in the back of my mind over possible health concerns, but her presence was intense and yet calming at the same time. She was confident, serene, and ever so intuitive. I could feel her resiliency and confidence beaming through me, and I just knew everything would be amazing with this little soul. When Emma was born, the nurses laid her in my arms, and she was very quiet. The doctor said, "Oh my goodness, she's not even crying. We've never seen such a calm baby." I looked at my husband, and we both wept, knowing she was a special soul, sent just for us.

My sweet Emma is four years younger than my beloved Benjamin. And even though I never got to meet my first, innocent, unborn baby, I believe he was sent to gently remind me to never take the blessing of motherhood for granted. My body did not fail me, it guided me with a blessing that I will never forget: everything happens exactly when it needs to, and not a moment sooner.

I am proud of my body for creating, carrying, and baring two sweet souls who will inevitably change the world. After my children were born, I found my old doll Adam in a box of childhood memorabilia in the basement. I was pleasantly surprised to see him still dressed in his little blue shirt and cloth diaper, and so happy to share him with my kids.

Let me tell you a little more about Benjamin: He is an old soul. With his mature language yet childish heart, he radiates pure innocence. Boyhood is fiercely calling him, and I often watch him learn how to be himself. I adore everything about him: who he is becoming, the dreams he believes in, and the man he will someday become. As I am his loudest cheerleader, he is my biggest fan. We hug and embrace, but I am never the first to let go. I am mindful to always take his gentle lead and respect his growth.

I smile bravely as he grows independent and earns freedom that my heart just isn't ready for. At times I see him watching the older boys in our neighborhood with admiration in his eyes, trying so hard to get their attention if only for a minute. I hear his little voice shaking. "Hi. My name's Ben, what's yours?" Such a sweet little voice. He's still so innocent. Learning, teaching, observing, adapting, changing—he's conquering this game of life. He laughs so loudly and loves so fiercely. He hugs so tightly and gives thanks so quietly. I watch him, we all watch him, teaching those around him, making kindness a priority, and embracing every chapter on his journey with wide, open arms.

He is resilient beyond belief, wise beyond his years, and ever so handsome. He is well-organized, a methodical planner, yet simultaneously spontaneous, funny, and extroverted at the same time.

He unknowingly wears his heart on his sleeve and continues to teach me to embrace this beautiful life. I am forever grateful for the moment we began this journey together. Just as I created him, he created me as a mama. He is my favorite and beloved boy.

As for my daughter Emma Skye, she is my spiritual teacher. She has soulful eyes and a gentle touch. If there is anything I can count on to be consistent in this life, it's the fact that Emma will tell me she loves me multiple times each day. She is lovable, huggable, intuitive, and ever so innocent. Animals love being around her, and birds sing in her presence. She notices everything: "Mumma, an airplane!" "Mumma, the trees are dancing!" "Mumma, the kitty is purring and that means he's happy." She is detailed and exceptionally appreciative of the little things in life.

Emma teaches everyone around her by exuding confidence, patience, and strength. She is beautiful in a soulful way; the kind of beauty that shines through her eyes.

She is also powerful, resilient, kind, and very perceptive. She is the most confident and secure being I have ever known. Emma gently guides me to be kind and open to others every day, whether we're in the store or at the park.

We were in the car one day, stopped at a red light in the city, idling next to a man who appeared very sad, unwashed, and holding up a cardboard sign that read: "Please help, anything will help."

As I was watching the traffic light, I saw the man waving in my peripheral vision. I looked in my rearview mirror and saw Emma (two years old at the time) waving at this man and smiling. No words were exchanged, and none were needed. When the light turned green, I peered over at him and he turned his sign over to the opposite side. It said: "Thank you."

I looked in my rear view mirror again and numerous realizations flooded my mind: Emma did not see a homeless man or a man begging for money; she simply saw a man. She was kind and gentle, and forced me to be as well. She is my favorite, sweetest, and honest girl.

Children respond to our fear, our teachings, and our judgments. They are not born hating or judging one another. Let's remember that our jobs as teachers and role models are important, but let's allow our children to teach us as well with their quiet guidance and genuine kindness. Allow your children to reveal their teachings, for they hold the best lessons.

→ Embrace motherhood ←

Learn from the children who are graciously placed in your life. At times, your job as a mama or papa might seem endless. Some of the daily routines often feel never-ending, leaving you dizzy like a hamster on a wheel and easily exhausted. We all-too-frequently spend our nights processing and analyzing our days as a parent, pondering what we may have done wrong, what we might need to do a little better, and truly hoping (fingers crossed) that no one judged our parenting style in public. We may even hope and visualize the adult versions of our children someday reassuring us that we did the best we could.

Instead of complaining about the many hats you wear as a parent (cook, maid, counselor, nurse, teacher), learn to shift your thinking a bit. Many of us get lost in our job description and forget to focus on the present moment. This moment will not last forever, remember that. Your children will not be little forever. There will be days when all seems lost and there is no end to the routine, and those are the days when you need to shift your focus. Start today. Focus on the small and simple things that make you smile. Make sure your little ones are safe, warm, loved and have full bellies. Learn to even embrace the ever-so-chaotic days, for those are the days you will recall later in life and smile about.

Take a few minutes each evening, perhaps as part of the bedtime routine, to reflect on your day with your children. Those few minutes are a wonderful way to fill their beautiful heads with good and comforting thoughts. Apologize if you weren't the best teacher or leader; you are, after all, only human. You can even simply ask, "Is there anything you want to talk about?" Use those minutes to quietly tell your children how much you love them. Praise them for all their good choices and listen to their sweet voices. Process, encourage, and snuggle. Leave quietly and calmly, while they descend to dreamland, feeling like the divine magical beings that they are.

I often feel the hustle and bustle with my own children: after school routines, reading lessons, school activities, and rushing around. As I stand in the midst of this chaos, it suddenly hits me: I am doing this. This is life. My children will remember these moments. We are so much more than "just a mama" or "just a papa." We are everything to those children.

As a parent, you are doing the most difficult yet gratifying job in the world; we all are. So let's love and support one another. On good days, bad days, and in-between days.

Don't compare parenting styles, disciplinary techniques, or breast-feeding choices. Just support one another. You never know who has suffered a loss, buried their child, or miscarried. Say a prayer for these triumphant women who are resilient, strong, and beautiful. Let's help one another and lift each other up. We are all unique mamas and papas. I am convinced that even on our worst days, we are exactly what our children need.

Lesson 5

Know your worth

Embrace courage

"Someone I once loved gave me a box full of darkness. It took me years to understand that this, too, was a gift."
—Mary Oliver

Regret is often the result of a dreadful decision we have made in the past, or a particular event that was out of our control, which left us with feelings of remorse.

People often say we should live life without regret, and the only way to do that is to learn from our mistakes; to gain wisdom and prosper with knowledge. Then we can even provide guidance to others who are experiencing similar challenges.

Unfortunately, we all have regrets in some domains of our lives. Upon reflection, however, you might just discover a few teachings hidden in those experiences that explain your current situation in life.

Shortly after my father's death, I became miserable and needy. I started craving the darkness and sadness because it somehow comforted me. We've all had moments of darkness in our lives, but it's not a place we can occupy for long. In an effort to fill the gaping hole deep within me, I threw myself into a romantic relationship, but I did it with my eyes closed and my heart already broken. This man entered my life with bold, fierce presence, and the twisted journey began. I completely lost myself when I was with him, and I lost my voice.

Allowing him to treat me unkindly served as a massive teaching moment in my life. He was dominant with a charismatic way of making me feel less important. He slowly convinced me that *his* needs were a priority, *his* job was better, and *his* way was the *only* way. There were times when I honestly believed that without him I would miserably fail in life. But my heart had a hard time reconciling the fact that just because I *tolerated* certain behaviors, didn't mean I actually *deserved* them.

After a year of things being rocky between us, we were standing in the kitchen one morning when he casually looked up at me and said, "What would you do if we broke up? Where would you go?"

I felt sick to my stomach. I was shocked, confused, completely dumbfounded, and deeply disturbed by his words.

"I don't have any plans for what I would do without you or where I would go." I replied. "You *are* my plan!"

My mind raced aimlessly. Did I need a backup plan? Why would he ask me such a question? Why would he put that awful thought in my head?

That morning was the beginning of seeing him in his true light, the beginning of my new reality, and the realization that my life could not be planned in advance. Ultimately, that morning was the beginning of *me*, learning the hard way, to embrace change.

I cried a lot and asked a thousand questions, but I received very little from him in return. He simply and calmly said to me, with little empathy and a fiercely cold tone,

"Things change, Jess. I'm changing, and I want you to be prepared that something may happen. Just be prepared, that's all."

This was a man to whom I was giving my all. I was planning my life with him and supporting his dreams. I immediately blamed myself, wondering what I had done to repulse him. What was wrong with me? Who did he want me to become? Was I really that hard to love?

Every night on my commute home from the office, I visualized us having a decent, adult, loving conversation, one that would end with hugs, kisses, and apologies. But every night I was greeted with, "I don't feel like talking tonight. Maybe tomorrow night."

All I wanted was to know what he was thinking about, what he felt was missing from his life, or what it was he so longed for that I wasn't giving him. It ate at my soul, painfully chipping away at my spirit. His words stabbed my heart, and his lack of commitment was turning me into someone I didn't even recognize.

I was always "too much" for him: too sensitive, too quiet, too organized… even my voice was too "childlike" for him. I was either "too much" of one thing or "not enough" of something else: not funny enough, not active enough, not social enough, not creative enough, etc.

With time I started realizing that I should never be too much or not enough of anything for someone who truly loves and appreciates me. I longed for the day when someone would look at me and say, "You're amazing just the way you are."

I reached a breaking point one night where I was so physically and mentally tired of the push-and-pull of our relationship, and I hit a whole new low for me: I begged. I literally sat on the floor beside the brown chair he always occupied, and I cried, "Please don't do this. I don't know what I've done wrong but I will change. I'll do anything to not have our lives shaken up and our dreams crushed. I don't know what I did, but I'm sorry. I'm so scared."

He just said, "Get up. Stop. I just wish you were more like… never mind… I'm just changing, and I don't want to talk right now."

That was the lowest point in my life, the most vulnerable I had ever felt. Imagine being stripped naked, shivering, cold, and helpless, forced to be strong where the only way out is up. It was like sweating and freezing at the same time. My body was trying to purge all the hurt and toxins with tears. So many tears. That was my loneliest moment, as I watched my little world crumbling down. I begged, I groveled, I cried. And then I stopped. Just like that.

I caught a reflection of myself in the window and saw a desperate, inconsolable woman on the floor. And I hated that woman. Who had I become?

Wiping the tears away from my cheeks, I picked myself up off the living room floor and walked to the bedroom. I lay quietly in bed, and started contemplating love. What am I trying to save here? An abusive relationship? A man who is infatuated with playing mind games? A person who didn't even flinch when I was on my knees, crying and sobbing? It hit me hard the next morning, how heartless and sad our life really was.

But days turned into weeks, and weeks turned into months, while all the signs that he was being unfaithful were there (like not coming home at night, hiding his phone, not introducing me to his friends), and I ignored all the red flags.

I blindly trusted him. I blindly praised him. I blindly *loved* him.

I can't recall when or why, but the spark between us faded. My heartache for him reminded me of when I was a little girl and I would pick the petals off of a daisy flower saying, "He loves me. He loves me not. He loves me. He loves me not." This little childhood ritual was actually a pure and accurate representation of our relationship: sheer confusion.

I convinced myself that he would change, decided to stay for a few more months, and to apply the hard work that our relationship clearly needed. Our days were either extremely great or unbearably terrible; there was no middle ground. I would watch him pull out of the driveway and see him smile, still loving his life as he was pulling away from our world together. And that became more and more apparent to me: a clear lesson that love cannot be forced, demanded, or manipulated. After months of feeling like I was the only one working on "us," I began to feel this intense urge to make a choice. I was simply too young to settle and remain unhappy for the rest of my life. He was not going to change, and he was never going to respect, support, or love me.

Delaying the inevitable, we started sleeping in separate rooms, dreading having to face each other over our morning routines before work.

Nestled next to my cat and crying in bed one Friday night, I suddenly looked up. I hadn't prayed in years. I didn't even remember how to pray or who I'd be praying to. But as foreign and yet familiar as it was, I closed my eyes and said, "Please… If I am meant to leave him and move on, just give me a sign. Give me some assurance that if I leave him I will be okay. I need to know I will be safe, happy, and loved somewhere else. I am miserable. I deserve so much more than this. I can't take it anymore. Please, just let me know."

The next morning I woke up feeling like I had just been handed a million dollars. I will never, ever forget that feeling. I got dressed, walked down the hall, and said, "Good morning. I'm going for a run; I feel amazing!"

The look of shock and confusion on his face was priceless. The tables turned. I had miraculously found my voice and wasn't afraid anymore. I felt a push from somewhere gently guiding me: "It's okay, honey, go. You can do this."

I felt supported, led, and ever so confident. As I ran that morning, I looked at the ocean and exhaled a huge sigh of relief. I called a girlfriend and said, "That's it… I'm taking my life back. I'm ending this relationship right now."

My heart was racing and I felt alive, as if a bright light was helping me find my voice, recognize my worth, and love myself again. I no longer felt like this man's property, his puppet, or an item he could place on a shelf and take down whenever he felt like it. This was *my life*. And I was going to find my happiness.

And then began the journey back to *me*.

We can't control love or ensure that it will last forever. Love *means* a taking a chance. Why people choose to intentionally cause heartache to one another will forever remain a mystery to most of us. Although I will never fully understand why people are unfaithful, I believe there is a lesson to be a learned from every relationship, even disloyal ones.

Falling apart was a blessing in disguise, as it forced me to put my pieces back together the way I actually wanted them to be. Walking away and not knowing what was on the other side was my biggest fear. Little did I know that the entire world was there, just waiting for me.

This man has crossed my mind during reflective meditation a few times over the years, and I often wonder if he has finally found his happiness. I have grown to understand and admire his spirit of inquisitiveness, and I can now appreciate his sense of adventure and resistance to routine. He was always so curious, so intensely full of wonder about what was on the other side of the fence. I can't hate him for that. He tried hard to fit into the mold that society has made for him, but he simply wasn't built for that way of life. He was bold and fearless, and I have grown grateful for his lessons. He was a beautiful example of embracing change, carrying with him lessons to celebrate individuality and live boldly. He didn't love the whole me, and that's okay, because it was the beginning of my own learning to love my whole self.

→ Embrace courage ←

Learn from your past relationships, and embrace the valuable lessons with gratitude and no regrets. Why? Because the person you were with was not only exactly what you wanted at some point in your life, but precisely who you needed as well.

When a chapter comes to a close, take time to process, reflect, and release. View closure as a time to grow, to learn, and to shine light on exactly what it is you need to understand about yourself.

Every partner, every encounter, and every relationship was no accident; they were meant to be—whether as a helper, a change agent, a light, or a lesson. We often curse our past and consider the amount of time we invested in those relationships misspent (mainly because we are angry, hurt, or embarrassed). But even though it may release some pain, try to avoid placing blame on the situation.

Time spent blaming others or focusing on the negative does not grant you access to the lesson buried within. You attract who you need at each moment in your life, and the lessons you are ready to learn so you can grow. It's all part of the journey. Your journey. So embrace the past, the partners, and the relationships by being grateful for the lessons, and kindly move on. You won't only feel lighter, but actually be excited for more opportunities to learn.

We all have that moment when we suddenly realize we've made a bad decision. Every single one of us has been in that situation. Sometimes it's unclear how we ended up there, or question how we missed all the red flags, but there is no need for blame or shame. No regret or guilt is required. Gently listen to your gut feelings and engage in pure reflection. The recognition of that moment is the first step to a new beginning. Rest assured that closing a chapter with a partner does not close the entire chapter of your future.

Embrace new beginnings, new opportunities to love, and a chance to redefine your future. Know that you are worthy, that your voice matters, and that you are valuable. Let love in by forgiving your past relationships and recognizing your astonishing value.

You are so worthy—worthy of love, devotion, and kindness. Go out there and find your happiness!

Lesson 6

Give yourself permission to love from afar

Embrace understanding

"It happens to everyone as they grow up. You find out who you are and what you want, and then you realize that people you've known forever don't see things the way you do. So you keep the wonderful memories, but find yourself moving." —*Nicholas Sparks*

Most of us take pride in the way we carry ourselves through life, and yet the way we see ourselves and the way we are perceived by others tends to be vastly different.

71

We are typically confident about a few of our traits, but there are also areas of buoyancy with which we may not connect until a challenge forces us to. We go through life wearing labels and carry ourselves at a certain "rank," often completely unaware that we are doing this.

"He's the funny one…" "That's the rude neighbor…" or "She's always late…" We are routinely categorized through life, but most of us don't know our own "status" or "title," which is a reflection of how the outside world perceives us. The challenge is to not get hindered by the label, but to stay connected to your true self. It takes a lot of energy to convince someone that you are *you* and not something they have predicted or expected.

There are also social and ownership statuses, such as "That's his wife" or "She's his little sister." In fact, when I was growing up, very few people referred to me by name; I was always "Little Doiron." People knew my older sister, and I seemed to have obtained a label that wasn't very individual. The challenge was learning to grow, to expand, and to individualize myself so that people would see *me* and not my label.

I was visiting my mother recently, and after a lovely dinner together, we sat down to watch an old, home movie of our family on her VCR. The tape was labeled, "The Doirons 1990."

There we were, on the big screen, our little family, and just like that we were instantly and completely transported to that time in our lives. Watching ourselves in a movie that was recorded 26 years ago was surreal. My mom said, "Honey, I'm your age there in the video, and you are the same age as your son is now. Wow!"

We could hear the man's voice behind the camera; my dad, narrating ever so smoothly, grammatically correct, and very soft spoken. About half way through the movie, after a Girl Scout ceremony, the footage switched to our home environment. My parents were in the military and all we ever knew was military base housing. So when we finally bought our family home that was off base in the late 1980's, it was magical. My father was in heaven with his little place to lay roots in the northernmost corner on the U.S. map: the tip of Maine.

We watched the video of my family celebrating birthdays, summer sprinkler fun, and Christmas decorating.

On the screen we looked like a picture-perfect family, and it truly felt that way when we were watching it. Only at the end of the movie did my dad make an appearance on the screen. He set that huge video recorder on its trusty tripod and recorded "Christmas of 1990." He was so happy. So proud. He was truly engaged, totally present in that very moment. No distractions, no posting to social media, no competition; just us in that moment of time. To see him and my entire family together, laughing, talking, smiling—it was blissful.

Were times simpler back then? I'm not sure. Every generation, every decade has its faults and trials. Being raised in a military family and having to maintain a certain image overrode any feelings of apprehension. I remember my parents telling us not to air our dirty laundry when we were growing up. My father would say, "Jess, that doesn't need to be shared with anyone. Do you want people thinking you're less than great?"

People would come visit and say things like , "Wow, Bob, you have it all—a beautiful wife, two wonderful girls, your own house… well done!" And he would beam with pride.

Families are interesting aren't they? Two people come together because of certain circumstances, decide to procreate, and are then forever tied to one another. Every family is unique, whether you like it or not. I was raised with a mom and a dad, and they had two children. My sister and I lived in the same house together, were raised with the same rules, and shared a room for many years, but we could not be more different in our personalities, beliefs, morals, or love languages.

My parents raised us to always feel "comfortable." And by "comfortable" they meant we don't speak of certain family members or situations that are difficult. If a family member was frowned upon, they were rarely spoken of, and when they were brought up in conversation, I remember feeling immediately awkward. My parents were adamant about keeping adult issues out of our childhood. As a kid, I never knew how much money my parents made, and I never had to worry about what was out of my control. I was a child and did child-like things: I played outside, got dirty, rode bikes, and played Nintendo.

I was never witness to gossip or drama in our home because it was always... *comfortable*. We spoke of "my dad's side," "my mom's side," "the ones we don't talk about," and "the family friends." I was ultimately taught, inadvertently, where each of our family members fit in. I can recall hearing an uncle's or cousin's name and immediately slotting them into one of those categories. As I grew older and learned more about my family members, I found myself gravitating toward the uncle around whom my father felt uncomfortable, yet growing distant from some of the celebrated friends of the family because I felt something was "off" about them.

It's hard growing up. You are told who to listen to, who to admire, who to avoid, and who to love. You are even disassociated from certain family members just because your parents have disengaged from them.

I remember graduating from high school and setting a personal goal to learn about my family members on my own. I wanted to ask them questions, feel their energy, hear their stories. I basically wanted to unlearn everything I heard about them growing up. Not because what my parents had taught me about them was wrong, but to discover them on my own, without any preconceived judgments.

As we continued watching the home movie from 1990, I found myself growing dismal, seeing our family on the big screen, completely blind to the changes that lay ahead.

I have remained close with some of my family members over the years, yet grew distant from others. There is a woman I adored as a child, but we have not spoken in many years. Drama became her comfort zone, her safe place, and I simply could not be part of the hurt anymore. I believe people only change when they choose to, it's that simple. She always had intense sadness in her eyes; lost and confused in her own skin. She mistreated and hurt me, lied endlessly, and left me feeling unworthy. But I kept putting time and energy into the relationship because she was "family."

It wasn't until I became a mama myself that I realized this mistreatment needed to stop. The drama, the abuse, the emotional head games—it all needed to stop. I had to shift my perspective and thoroughly analyze where my love and energy were going.

If this woman was just a friend, not a family member, I would have stopped talking to her years ago. If a coworker mistreated me like this, I would disengage and walked away. So why was I willing to accept and condone an abusive relationship simply because she was family? People should not be given a free pass to hurt you just because they are related.

I struggled with the decision to disengage for years; it weighed heavily on me. But the sinking feeling I had in my stomach every time I spoke to her, and the way I couldn't share happy news with her because of her intense judgment and hurtful responses, lingered in my mind. How could I sit with my own children and tell them that bullying is wrong, teach them how anger is hurt's bodyguard, encourage them to always disengage when conflict arises, and then not take my own advice? What kind of example would I be setting? It was time I recognize my own worth. So I began to slowly distance myself, started loving her from afar, and began the work of forgiving what I needed to forgive.

No label gives you the right to mistreat, to abuse, or to lie to anyone. I realized I was allowing her to treat me this way because she was family. It is never okay to be cruel to someone, no matter the circumstances. You can't fix people, and you can't have others see the world through your eyes.

Sometimes the best thing to do is wish them well and love them from afar. You may not always understand the life path that others are on, but you can always choose to send love and understanding out into the world.

⟶ Embrace understanding ⟵

Learn the love language of your family. Participate in family gatherings, respect your family values, and carry on the family traditions. Learn and understand, however, that it may be necessary to gently break negative patterns and start loving certain family members from afar.

Listen to your elders' gentle guidance about family members, but explore your relatives on your own as well. Allow each individual to share their own story, and then sit with how it feels. Think of someone who has challenged you, hurt you, betrayed you, saddened or misunderstood you. Think of that person. Think of the feelings you have tied to that person. Do the feelings linger? Do the feelings sit unsettled in your stomach? Do you instantly feel your heart race? These are all signs that you need to forgive, accept the situation, and move forward.

Forgive the situation and the person in order to free yourself, and then think of this person in a new, warm light. The ability to see them from a new perspective is a sign that you are forgiving them. Think of one positive quality about this person, and let that quality shine. There is good in everyone. And there is a lesson in every hurtful situation.

Focus on the lesson, the warmth, and the good instead of the hurt. Today, send that person some loving, kind thoughts, and be comfortable with wishing them well from afar. Keep moving forward on this amazing journey with nothing holding you back.

There will be some people in your life who need to be loved from afar; not everyone is healthy or kind enough to deserve a front row seat in your life. Allow others to act as they will, but do not sink to their level. Remember to always respond with kindness. React with love. Always.

What you say about others while they are not around says a lot about who *you* are. Be sure to respect your tribe, your family, and your loved ones. If you find the energy in a room you're in turning negative about someone you admire, gently disengage.

Disengage when it comes to gossip and negative conversation about others, especially family. Lay your head on the pillow at night with ease, knowing you truly love and respect others.

You are not the labels that others assign to you. People who choose to label you and not see your greatness do so from a place of fear. Do not live in fear. Build one another up and create an energy that is individual and confident. Understand that you will not always comprehend everyone's unique journey or the choices they make. Misunderstanding, confusion, and disagreements happen all the time. These are not reasons to think or speak ill of someone.

The way you live your life is individual and unique, as it should be. You do not need to defend, explain, or prove anything to anyone; you only need to *be*. Just be. Don't carry hatred in your heart; it will only limit your potential and dim your own light.

Understand that others have their own journey and their own lessons to learn. Set clear boundaries, know your worth, and have compassion for others who are projecting pain and unhappiness. Send only love and understanding out into the world.

Lesson 7

Believe in love

Embrace change

"A soul mate won't let you hide your darkness, a soul mate will bring it to the surface so it can be healed."
—*Mastin Kipp*

He is a warmhearted man who shows me authentic and honest love, consistently reminds me of my worth, and treats me with respect, dignity, and honor.

He is a true and wise soul, with beautiful values deeply ingrained in his core to provide-for and protect his family. With a calm demeanor that radiates great humility, he expresses gratitude every single day. He is my teacher, my calm presence, and my support.

Immensely confident in his own skin, his presence is overwhelmingly inspiring. He sets goals and succeeds at attaining a sense of purpose in life, with an amazing work ethic, quiet demeanor, and calm energy. A truly humble man whose simple presence is grounding, he is the most kind and supportive friend I have ever known. He is my person. He is my one true love. He is my husband.

We first met in my office, over ten years ago, on a bright and sunny day. There were two chairs in the waiting room, and he occupied one of them, dressed in khaki pants and a pale, blue, button-up shirt. He stood up as soon as I walked in, hand extended, and calmly yet confidently introduced himself. I will never forget the feeling that traveled through my soul, like a bolt of electricity pulsating every nerve in my body. My mouth went dry, my heart started racing, and time seemed to briefly stop. I was transported back to the ninth grade, feeling like I just found a note in my locker from my crush. It was intense. Were we twin flames? Soul mates? Familiar friends? I wasn't quite sure. I just knew it felt comfortable. He felt comfortable. It was genuine soul recognition.

As much as everything seemed electrified and flustered, it simultaneously felt calming, tranquil, and peaceful. Our interaction was honest and easy. We were both in committed relationships with longtime partners at the time, and we met under casual, business circumstances, but the unexpected connection between us made me question everything.

I was the woman who mapped out her entire life and took pride in planning every event, every milestone, every encounter. I believe this was the universe giving me a gentle, serendipitous message: you cannot plan for everything, my dear, you and this man will love each other on a soulful level… you'll see.

Over the next few months we had several business meetings. I kept my strong feelings hidden because I did not fully understand them nor wish to explore them further at the time. I couldn't comprehend the magnetic pull, the comfort I felt with this complete stranger, or the intense feeling of warmth when he was around me. Weeks turned into months, and months turned into years. In fact, four years passed, during which we each started a family, but then we both unwittingly ended our previous relationships at the same time.

One day, on my morning commute to work, I turned on the radio and heard a familiar voice. His voice.

Later that day, between client meetings, a coworker and I decided to look him up on social media, and there he was, staring back at me on the screen. The warm feelings came flooding right back, my stomach started aching with nervousness, and I was excited just looking at his picture. Weeks went by before I finally worked up the courage to send him a message:

"Hi! How are you? I hope you're doing great. You may not remember me…"

"Hi! Of course I remember you. How are you?"

"I cannot believe I found you after all these years. Can I ask you a question?"

"Sure, ask away."

"Okay, are you seeing anyone?"

"Oh no, not at all. Please don't tell me you want to set me up with someone. I hate dating. Who are you asking for?"

"I'm asking for me. :)"

"Oh, well that's wonderful. I'm all in ;)"

And away we went. We spent hours on the phone and I couldn't wait to see him, to touch his face, to watch his mannerisms, and to smell his aroma. I was head over heels for this man even when I barely knew him. We constantly sent emails and text messages to one another, and once we each settled-in for the evening after work, we spoke endlessly on the phone. There were even a few conversations during which I peered over and saw 4:16 a.m. on the clock. I would drag myself to work the next day like a zombie, but I was so high on this man. It was amazing.

No one had ever spoken to me with such love and genuine kindness before. He complimented every aspect of my being, and was immensely honest about his feelings for me. He was truly proud to be with me.

We were honest with each other from the very beginning, never feeling the need to hide anything or to put up any walls. We disclosed our secrets and talked about our pasts, fully accepting one another. Never questioning, never judging, simply viewing our past challenges as learning curves and stepping stones. We often discussed our sons, who were ironically only one month apart in age. We would talk about "our boys" and dream of our future, effortlessly falling deeper and deeper in love.

Three weeks went by, and we finally worked up the courage to meet face to face for the first time in four years.

We agreed to meet for dinner, and I was insanely nervous on the drive to the restaurant. I parked next to his SUV, stepped out of my car, and when he came around the side of his vehicle my cheeks began to ache from smiling so big. We hugged, drenching ourselves in that amazing moment. It was as if time stood still, and everything felt aligned, all at once.

He was a complete gentleman, extremely present, engaging in deep conversation, inquiring about my life and my dreams. He owned his identity and beamed with self-worth. He did not require constant reassurance or praise; he was simply looking to have me enhance his life. It was truly that simple. He was not looking for his "other half;" he knew he was already whole, and that was truly admirable—and extremely sexy.

Such a comfortable night between two people, as if we had been a couple our entire lives. It felt like our souls had known each other for years, but to the outside world we were newly dating. It was very difficult to capture or to describe to others what we had. Why should time be a measurement of love? As Tony Robbins so perfectly said, "You can be in a relationship for two years and feel nothing; and you can be in a relationship for two months and feel everything. Time is not a measure of quality, of infatuation, or of love."

Nothing was planned between us. Nothing was "normal" about how we met or reconnected, or how we would eventually become a blended family. And none of this was "the old me."

I had carefully scheduled everything in my life before this: my college graduation, my previous long relationship, my pregnancy, my career, even weekly dinner menus. (Okay, I still plan weekly dinner menus.) But with him, everything was chaotic yet comforting, crazy yet calming, sensitive yet sexy as hell. I was *me* when I was with him. Completely, unapologetically me. And it felt amazing.

Everything happened quickly, but it felt so right. Within a year we moved in together, got engaged, bought a house, and got married. People constantly asked, "Do you really want to rush into things?" "Why not just take your time?" "Are you sure this is the right thing to do?"

Opinions... so many opinions.

Our thoughts and feelings were not going to be hindered or influenced by what others considered "the right way." He and I had been in previous relationships where we had done things "the right way," and we'd been miserable. We were going to do what felt right and do things *our way*.

Seven years in, we are still completely and utterly in love with the perfectly imperfect life that we have co-created.

Everyday challenges and complications seem a bit lighter when your partner has your back. At times, I am proud of myself for not slipping back into old habits and questioning everything: his motives, kindness, genuine heart, or his sincere approach to life—what would that accomplish? Nothing.

He didn't hurt me in the past. He didn't cause the scars or mistrust. He came into my life bringing honest love and pure light. I had to shift my perspective, condition my mind, and alter my focus to remind my entire being that he did not hurt me. Someone who didn't know how to love hurt me. I needed to be open to real love. Open to receiving love. His love.

When I stopped blaming others for one bad relationship, there was an entire world out there that was full of love, trust, and guidance just waiting to be experienced.

You *can* love again. You *can* trust again. Don't categorize all men or all women just because one person hurt you. Learn the lesson, close the chapter, and gently move on. Know that true, mindful love is waiting for you. Mindful love is all-inclusive and worthy of the risk. *Trust me.*

My favorite thing to say to him is, "It's so easy to love you." He brings balance to my life by kindly reassuring me, "It's all right, love; it always works out." And it honestly does.

I've never witnessed such ease and comfort in a relationship before. It's as if every challenge or change presented to us is calmly driven in the right direction by some force greater than either one of us, gently whispering, "It's okay, you two, you got this. Nothing can ruin you. See, I told you that you'd be great together."

⇢ Embrace change ⇠

Learn that love is all around. Love doesn't hurt. Love is bravery. Do you realize how brave you are for opening your heart to others? Love is honesty and pure vulnerability. We've all been hurt and scarred, yet we continue to have this ability to love again. Regardless of how many times your heart has been broken, it always has more to give. It takes strength and courage to put love out there, to put your heart on the line, to invest love in another human being, and allow the space for someone to love you back. It's really remarkable.

We are all just human beings wishing we could expose our souls and communicate to others what we actually want and need from one another. Be your own *whole* best friend. You are already whole. You are already complete. Relationships are not 50/50, they are 100/100. You are not half of anything. You are a beautiful, unique, inspiring soul that is already whole and complete in this very moment.

Be open to all encounters because you never know when or where your soul mate will appear; a sporadic conversation at a coffee shop, the time you skipped a planned event and ended up meeting someone while waiting for a slice of pizza, or when you take a chance on a new hobby and it becomes your passion. No moment or serendipitous encounter is ever random. Our lives may feel unpredictable, but they are divinely created with intention. Remain grounded, stay focused, just be in this moment. Be open and attentive to what life may bring onto your path. It takes only one tiny second, one single moment, for someone to enter your life and beautifully revise your original plan.

Gently remind yourself, every single day, of what you are and what you are not: You are not your faults; you are a beautiful soul on a learning journey. You are not the opinion of someone who chooses to judge you; you are an independent warrior, and you know that what others think about you is none of your business. You are not damaged goods or broken from life's lessons; You are experienced, knowledgeable and open to growth. You are not unworthy, unlovable or undesirable; you are a beautiful, unique soul, and no one else can play your part. You are not a failure; you are the successful outcome of the lessons presented to you.

Please know that you are powerful. You have survived every lesson presented to you, every storm, every chapter—and you are still here. Share your story. Trust your journey. Learn the lessons by embracing change.

About the Author

Jessica E. Smith is the founder and owner of *Embrace Change* (EmbraceChangeInLife.com), a beautiful mix of learning how to persevere through positive affirmations and self acceptance. Jessica is committed to helping people find the blessing in every experience, no matter how bad that experience may seem. Her mission is to help others learn how to accept change, live without fear, and promote self care.

Jessica has created a strong community of grace and motivation through her meaningful writing and strong presence on social media, modeling ways to embrace change. Her work has been wildly published, and she holds many titles including wife, mother, writer, gardener, pianist, entrepreneur, inspirational speaker, and private self-care coach. Raised in Maine, Jessica enjoys the Maine way of life with her husband and two kids.

She holds a bachelor's degree in rehabilitation services and experience that only eight years in the social work field can bring, including behavioral strength-based modification and crisis intervention. Jessica is passionate about gently guiding others to recognize their worth, embrace their journey, and share their story.

Acknowledgments

⇥ Gratitude and love ⇤

I would like to honor and express my deepest appreciation for my parents, Candina and Robert, who showed me unconditional love, support, guidance, and discipline; my Nana Lucore, who taught me patience and the importance of a strong work ethic; my Uncle James and Aunt Victoria, who gently reminded me of my worth and continuously guide me. Thank you. Small family; big love.

I would like to express extraordinary love and affection for my husband, Corey. You are my safe place, my rock, my person. Thank you. I love your face, my handsome man.

I would like to lovingly recognize my two children, Benjamin and Emma, you are my turkey man and my pumpkin. You two guide me and are so easy to love.

I would like to express enormous appreciation to my beautiful niece, Ashlie. You have forever warmed my heart, and you will lovingly change the world. Forever grateful for our connection, my little version of me.

I would like to lovingly recognize my bonus son, Amos. You are an adventure and I am forever grateful for your little soul finding its way to me. Thank you, my little Batman.

I would like to extend immense gratitude and love to my soul sister tribe: Nicki Blackstone, Shelly Caldwell, Michelle Olsen, Nicole Zenga, Stephanie Wiehn, Krystal Malinovskii, Erin Peacock, Tracy Richardson, Amy Gagne, Jamie Caldwell, Michelle Goulet, Tina Constatine, Lisa Obery, Sharon Gagne. And a special thank you to my UMF soul sisters, who shone light on my darkest year: Angela VanDine, Erin York, Sarah Jamo, Molly Whitehouse.

I would like to express tremendous amounts of gratitude to my supporters, guides, and mentors: Colleen Smith, Canaan York, Nick Poitras, Jennifer Moore, Cheryl Begley, Joan and Bob LeBlanc, Chris Dumas, Lisa Greable, Raul Luna Jr., Darylen Cote, Jill Wheaton, Ryan Esbjerg, David and Elaine Donovan, Olivia Wright, Vadim Makhlis, Susan Mugford, Ron Gaudreau, Colin Staab, Kathy Eaton, AJ Dukette, Wendy Lamoreau, Sharon LeBlanc, Elna Joseph, Ann Quinlan; Arlene Kelley for her creative talents and artwork; and my exceptional English Composition professor at UMF, Kathleen Beaubien.

"The Seven Lessons is a must-read for every woman. This nonfiction book is deep, profound, insightful, and written with eloquence of a storyteller who reaches out to each reader through life experiences and real life challenges. This book is full of lessons and hope. Smith's optimistic view of each lesson is fueled by a mix of self-compassion, intelligence, and inner strength. She creates a sense of well-being and confidence in the reader that they too should never give up hope and never stop believing when they feel lost. This book is a gift for the heart and soul."

—*Michelle Goulet*

Founder,
Kidz Go Eco

"To some, the word 'lessons' from the title of this book may imply that Jessica's goal in writing it was to teach or perhaps even to lecture or preach. This could not be further from the truth. The Seven Lessons are not taught but rather passed on through Jessica's masterful and unbelievably honest storytelling. While many have written books about their own lives with the genuine goal of helping others, never before have I felt so inspired simply by reading someone's story. I did not feel as if the author's goal was to have me buy in to her point of view or learn anything specific from her experiences. Instead Jessica allows the reader to draw his or her own conclusions and to walk away changed in their own unique way. Bravo to Jessica for not only having the courage to open herself up to the world but also for doing it in a manner that I am certain will have a deep and profound impact on all that are fortunate enough to pick up this book."

—*Vadim Makhlis*

President and CEO,
Performance New England

"I was truly touched by the candor and authenticity in Jessica Smith's collection of stories. By offering her willingness to share experiences that are real and genuine, Jessica brings insight to our own stories and hope for the challenges we all endure. She takes us on a journey of personal discovery and grace.

Starting with a tender story of how pets teach us through their unconditional love, Jessica guides us even deeper with tales of friendship, vulnerability, sorrow, forgiveness, loss, appreciation, desperation, fortitude, honesty, perspective, courage, and gratitude. I am sincerely thankful to have had the privilege to read these moving stories, which offered me inspiration to keep showing up and embracing change in my own life."

—*Jennifer Elizabeth Moore*

Intuitive Mentor, Spiritual Healer,
and Creator of the Empathic Woman System

www.modernmedicinelady.com

CPSIA information can be obtained
at www.ICGtesting.com
Printed in the USA
BVOW08*0944251016

465710BV00006B/4/P